Dedicated to the women who wear the name Evans, the ones never asked and the ones who refused and carried our recklessness anyway.

CONTENTS

FOREWORD
by Hanif Abdurraqib

I find myself, then, considering fatherhood – despite not traveling towards it myself. Rather, upon finishing this book, I find myself considering what it is to love something so much that it becomes a part of you, or something that you would give a life for.

Will and I have taken similar paths to this work – the work, ultimately, of excavation as a means of both archival and survival. We're both black men from corners of Ohio where being black was sometimes a blessing and a curse. In my earliest days of writing poems, I would amble into the open mic night that Will ran and sit far in the back, sometimes with a shitty, crumpled-up poem in my pocket. Because I first became introduced to Will's work when he was already a titan of the local scene, I thought then as I do now: Will has never written a bad poem. I think there's some romantics involved in my imagining of this, but I became certain when reading *Still Can't Do My Daughter's Hair* that Will Evans has not only never written a bad poem, but he's done the hard work: He's found new ways to write the good poem. The hard poem, especially.

I don't say this to say that Will has been a father to me, of course. Romantics aside, I wouldn't burden him with that. But what Will has been to me is a mentor, which is a type of irreplaceable relationship that echoes the gentleness and care that exists in this book. Not only did Will care for my poems and my growth as a poet, he taught me how to care for the growth of others. In this way, we are a part of each other's lineage, and are crafting an entire generation in that mold.

And yet what grasps me about this book is that Will, for the first time in his work, is grappling with a very palpable fear that is unfamiliar to me. Fear, that takes many forms: a needle in "Vaccines," for example, bringing back a childhood fear and giving it newer and better clothes. For the first time, our work feels somewhat disparate – a new ocean between our narratives. This, of course, draws me more eagerly to the landscape built. This is, more than anything, a book about women, isn't it? A book about the women who keep men alive, and the ones we want to survive for. There are so few good ways for men to write about women – time and time again, we've seen our imaginations fail to present a narrative for the women we love to live in as full and complex people. Will, in the way only his work can, finds the razor's edge, honoring the women in his life while still understanding that he is incapable of saving them.

So much of Will's work, when I first saw it and when people were first talking about it around me, was discussed through a lens of volume and physicality. Now, I say that this is something that befalls a lot of black poets who read their poems in a manner that won't put spectators to sleep. But it must be said that Will is, indeed, a performer who is capable of milking every ounce of feeling out of a room, and doing it by emotional force. Underneath it all, he is simply a storyteller. His work, always on the narrative path. Everything has a birth and rebirth. "Call the Gospel by Its Given Name," an origin story with a beginning, middle, and cliffhanger.

It is trite to say that all of these poems are angling towards death. I think what makes them work is what I've always admired about Will's poems and what has pushed me in learning from him: the awareness of death is a character in the poem. More than any actual person, there is the knowing that life is finite. What is urgency in a poem if there is nothing tethering the author to that which they deem precious? And, listen, I don't wanna die today, tomorrow, or the next day. But, shit – I sure know I might. And I've got to find out what of my legacy is gonna be left for anyone who loved me after I'm gone. And Will has maybe been figuring that out for a long time, but he doesn't do it any better than he does here. And I get it, everything is a cliché, right? But when I met Will, he wasn't a father and now he is. And I came up around a bunch of kids who claimed they had nothing to live for, and maybe some of them didn't. And so, what I'm saying is that once, I knew what it was to look for the light switch in a dark room and find nothing. And in this book, I am reminded of the moment when, by the mercy of another, you finally find that switch and the room floods with that which might blind you, but instead gives you a renewed purpose.

All of this is to say a simple thing: Will Evans is writing poems like he wants to be alive a little bit longer, even knowing that isn't promised. I think – for a person at the margins in this era or any era – that's all we can ask.

A lot of me, if I'm still being honest, is still a young poet with a crumpled poem in my pocket back at the Method Gallery on a Tuesday night, listening to Will read some of his work. It is amazing, really. The paths that people think they are building for us, when they're really building a path for themselves. I am proud of this book. I am proud of Will for writing the hard work, because I know that's what he would ask of me – today and always. Will's work, here and always, is the long hand reaching into the dark room and flicking on the lights.

STILL CAN'T DO
MY DAUGHTER'S HAIR

WILLIAM EVANS

DUST

If I say that I am an old man now,
what I mean is that my daughter
once pointed her finger at me
and yelled, *Bang, Daddy, you're
dead*, and I fell down in a heap
of my murdered youth and yelped
in theater to her giggling applause,
this time without tasting a friend's
blood spray against my profile or
feeling the weight of his expiration
fall against the summer of my fifteenth
year, no longer picturing the mural
of our collapse against the already
red brick wall of a school that he
never got to walk the halls of again.

FATHER / DAUGHTER

like the thrush
that returns to the fallen
tree, uproot and burden.
Abandoned earth in its leave.
Now quiet spectacle. Sap congealed
from its branches,
gnarled beneath the weight
of its body, fissures pecked
apart and breezy. Surely
the winged beetles,
snails easy to pull from
their armor, a slug pink
with finality, are worth
the tree's quietus?
The bird is a glutton.
The bird is not a vulture
but knows how to empty
a carcass. The worms almost escape
from her mouth, a partisan
wound. She hovers above the rot
wondering what is worth
remembering. The forest recedes
a little more each new sun.

The forest near our home
is a hollowed fruit, a starved
history. Ripe for fire, if nothing else.
Pine combs snap in succession
under my daughter's steps.
I mistakenly blame the ache
in my knees on old age. My daughter
plays among the ruins. I am a playground
of dead bark. Boughs that will never

flower, again. She asks me what
happened to this forest, but I cannot
tell her of how I was once sapling,
that she flourishes
in the splinters of me.
Or the splinters of a man, who was
once a boy that thought he
would live forever.

AURIBUS TENEO LUPUM

The archway above
the door of my daughter's new
school says something in Latin
about hard
work and leadership
but nothing about the tuition
fee required to walk through it.
The school is only new to us
as it has stood without us or people
that look like us
for decades,
and this is what my wife and I do
with our hard work and leadership;
a ransom we have secured,
we grease the rails for our daughter.
This is what you do
when you
are Black
and at jobs where you
suffer
through being
the minority,
you send your daughter
to the better
school where she
will suffer through being
the minority. But they love us
here. They love the shirt
and tie I pick as armor
to wear when I leave my daughter
with them. They love locks that twist
down my wife's back
like taut rope they can point

out to investors. *Your family is adorable,*
would you mind posing
for this picture, you know we are remaking
the flyer, can we put you on the cover?
Give us
your daughter, she was too smart
to stay wherever
you came from. See the community
we're building? See how
we have tamed the wild
dogs, I bet you haven't heard
one bark since you got here. We can't
guarantee they won't get
hungry if you leave.

JASMINE, WHEREVER

the girl who can't sit still, can't let the beat drop, can't let the night
fall upon us without a fight that invades bedtime asks me, almost
daily if we can have a dog. And her mother? Not much help.
She pretends that I am the one pulling the drawbridge on her best
ambitions, but no, it isn't like that. I just remember the last dog my
family had when I was younger when we didn't   know how
fractured we   were and my sister   loved on Jasmine

every   day, feeding   her as much   blood
and   bone as we   could   muster until

Jazz   ran   away and never
came back   because   who   wants
    to be   in a building   where
the   residents   pretend   to

not   see   the flames bursting
from its windows   until everything

    is light   and every   thing

has had   water   pulled
    from its   gasping   body
so I say   something   like
if you can settle   *down*
    for bed then maybe
I'll think about it even
though I think   about not
wanting   to be   abandoned
again
almost every day   why would I
    have my only family   now if
I didn't fear   the opening

of my veins
       and nothing
pouring   out from them
or the docility of my
body on the floor
of a vacant house like a man
that has watched history
invite itself
into the man's   home
and take
up all
the chairs

I TURN THE VOLUME DOWN BECAUSE BEYONCÉ SAYS FUCK WHILE I DRIVE MY DAUGHTER TO SCHOOL

The four-year-old gives her first protest of the morning
whether warranted or the default   position
of her mother's legacy. Her fist is balled the way a boy
would grip her hair in a kindergarten class   or at any age
that boys put
their name on things. She says, *hey I like that song*
and Beyoncé has already finished saying *I'm gonna fuck me up a*
bitch so I turn   the volume back up to five seconds ago before I
told this muse what
sound was too ripe for my daughter's lungs, before I   too
was a fist resting upon the speaker and I know
it doesn't take
much to get this little girl's blood
into a spell because it was once her grandmother's blood,
which means there will be a day when someone
some man tries to pull it out
of her and she   becomes a wound
where the curses her father hid from her come
tumbling out

WE MAKE A LIST FOR THE GROCERY STORE BECAUSE I'LL FORGET

The woman in line ahead of us at the grocery store
thinks my daughter is adorable because of course

she is and makes a joke about how it's going to
be a full-time job keeping the boys away from

her and I smile with more teeth than I actually
have and say, *something like that,* but she keeps

talking, now about how she might have to lock
her girls in their rooms until they go to college

because she doesn't want to be a grandmother
and I laugh mostly because I once became a girl's

first in the back of her silver Honda Civic, back
when we were both gorgeous and so afraid

of the present we decided to skip the last bits of
our childhood. And I say *girl* not to be cute, but

because I honestly don't remember her name.
But I do remember no one ever threatening to lock

me in a closet for fear that I might be too
loose of a star to stay lodged in the night sky.

Only thing anyone ever told me was *don't let no
girl trap you,* which might have meant that the girls

were teeth, only there to bleed me
and I should try to make it back home with nothing

attached to me, including the beasts themselves.
Guess I didn't know she might stop being someone's

daughter after she got my scent on her. Guess I
don't have enough shadow in me to blanket my

daughter in the shame of her own experience and call
that prayer fatherhood, and call that the last stand oath

of a man protecting no one except the wavy spines
of fragile men before him falling from under his tongue

VACCINE

I remove my shirt so
the nurse can give me
a flu shot and she preps
my arm with her fingers
pressed into my flesh
the way someone would firmly
press a doorbell, expecting
another to answer the summons.
She bares my shoulder while saying
my, you are a big one, aren't you.
My shoulder is a bronze
trophy in this nurse's fingers
and I wait for the needle, wondering
how many bucks heard the wind
whisper how gorgeous they
were through the trees
of a perilous forest
before it carried the first
bullet with it.

BIOLOGY

This one time in biology we were supposed
      to dissect frogs, but the shipment of dead
and preserved bodies didn't arrive on time, so I guess
      I, being the slender black boy, had to do.
The white girls giggled until the reaction bubbled over
      the glass lip and one of them
asked me what size shoe I wear. The giggle became
      a colony of metal instruments being dropped
into metal trays. The giggle was a formaldehyde
      headache where I coughed to remind them
I was still breathing. Someone dropped a scalpel
      on the floor and I flinched because I was always
in season. I was tense in fast-twitch muscle and good
      stock. I was alarmed, ready for market
and a deloused tongue. Good veins, pumping good
      boy in my hollows. My knee bobbing,
the calf muscle tight like a coiled escape. I tucked
      my shoes beneath my chair and noticed
that one of my size 13 NIKE Airs had a scuff
      mark on the heel. I couldn't keep the damn thing hidden
away. I didn't even notice
      that they had already pinned my arms and legs down to the
tray and begun to peel back my chest
      'til the lungs and heart and liver turned
brown from the exposure to air, no one wondering what
      pond I came from, how I was ever caught
or if my wide and blinking eyes were as big
      as everything else on me.

PACK

Because the Black girls don't usually say *cock*,
when the wolf says, *Why you actin' all scared*

to pull your cock out? I am gutted and opened
up onto the concrete. School has let out, all children

are gone or were never truly here. It is I
and the long-legged snarl with her palm up like a beggar

that greets me paws first. I am the boy who has already
decided to forsake himself. I know nothing of my father

or the sky I will no longer welcome through
my bedroom windows. I have surrendered my body

to the spear, do not recall cheap candy
cigarettes or cookouts with distant

family, or the feathered voice of my auntie
that once held me like a laugh that escaped from

her chest. No, I am fifteen and apologizing
for being a willing prey like a good bison

is supposed to be. Even as I pretend to not see
her friends giggling around the corner of the building.

Even as the tremor in my legs has stopped because I'm too
old for that now. Either this or she tells the older

girls how small I must be to hide myself within
myself. Either this or she may never like me.

When she puts me in her hands, I forget my mother's
name or the salty tears I once tasted or the thing

I wanted to become before I became the thing I never
planned on. And it's possible that I am ashamed

at my own arousal or scared at how well I can dig
a grave I know is meant for my own body,

how a girl's laugh will always sound
like a tongue cleaning my blood

from its teeth. Or I can't get over that she held me
like this for what must have been my best years,

until the pack had filled their stomachs with my kill
or until my ride came to pick me up and the girls

in the following years all became howls
in an unstill night I could never find true north in.

FOUND

After 2nd period, they gathered us
together like regrets to tell us J.R.
was found by the old tire depot and
the rest of the students paused long enough

to wonder if they were still serving pizza
at lunch. We didn't ask any questions about
J.R. or what jersey he rocked to his rubble deathbed
but someone said something about skipping

the next class and I was with it because that's world
history and I'd had my fill of kneeling into a text
where I didn't show up until the end, but really I needed time to tell
my best friend how the girl

in high school that used to babysit him
told me to come inside the house while her
mom was at work barely making enough to pay
for it. She didn't take her bra off, but instead curved

her fingernail around my bony ribs
as if she were peeling the freshly picked orange she
did not pay for and once our underwear
became orphans at the bottom of the bed,

she told me I would be a man today and I think
she meant that I was now the bullet that she had wrought
and all I needed was to beg where to be aimed. She
held my head as gentle as malice

shoved my voice into her like a shotgun. J.R. saw
the hunting knife before it took his last name
and wished to see his mom again. The hallways
at school forgot his scent, but could smell on my skin

a boy that had passed away.
I came home to a loud and empty
apartment and I might have cried about never
seeing J.R. again like I did

when they found the last boy last month,
but so much has changed since then.

THE BOYS RAN PAST AND THE FLOWERS
NEVER GREW BACK

say a prayer for my father
who art not in heaven yet
who wore an afro like a
life vest in service of the akron
flood. it claim a family every
summer, every day in north
ohio be a coming of age story
be the beginning of a blood oath
you redeem in another part of
the lower forty-eight. praise be the zero
year, praise the artist that gets your
baby hair just right on the cover
every black boy gets a grand exit
they don't all get origin stories,
unless you count the first time
they got called a nigger. first time
their name is split over the molars
of a man in a uniform and spit out
like church wine. we hitchcock,
shoot our love scenes like murders,
and who among us ain't dreamt of
their body draped in lights and making
a beautiful exit wound to a paying crowd?
they say all the brothas round my way
are great storytellers. no, we just
remember every color of the thing
that tried to kill us. want to hear a joke:
nobody i know lost their virginity
on lover's lane blvd, but the crips
used to set up shop there,
until someone decorated the street
with kevin's body. left him in the weeds

until the roses fermented
around his head. not funny? maybe
i gotta work on my timing. give me death or
give me death where my mama
doesn't have to appear on cnn. we just
boys in the snapbacks, got just enough
spanish in our throat to flirt with rosa
up the block or tell rosa's brother
how the security guard at the mall
groped her when they said she
stole something. maybe a body without
puncture is too big of an ask. maybe we start smaller;
maybe we just want somebody to
see us without imagining a future
without us. guess our love scenes stay
murder. rosa told a boy he
was fine like denzel and she never came
back from the party. guess the flood
can claim anyone, guess i still ain't funny.
still alive though. still working on
my timing.

SHELTER, MEANING OTHER PEOPLE

Nobody dare call BB a ho
to her face, even though
she done collected about six
of us pistols on the block.
Guess cuz she can ball with the dudes
or everybody scared of her brother.
But Terrell smacks her ass on the court
and keeps his teeth after, so we all know
why he wasn't hanging with us
last night, and I figure maybe I ain't
pretty enough, or it's because I can't dunk
yet like Terrell cuz all she ever do
in my direction is sweat and roll her
eyes when I try to dribble left, but it's towards
the end of the summer and everybody go
home after the last game, and BB ain't drive
today, so we walk back together,
her hand on my head the entire time
while she tells me how *niggas ain't shit*
but hoes ain't either, so be careful
and how one night she let Terrell
lay up on her and then cry
for an hour afterwards
because nobody at his house gave
a damn if he was coming home
or not.

CATCH AND RELEASE

Some girl asked me
how many girls I've
slept with and I answered
don't ask questions you
don't want to know
the answer to
but I could fill a woman
with all the shit I don't
actually know. Every part
of me is worn soil
that needs to be tilled until
I am worthy of oranges again.
I once loved a woman so
intensely she placed me inside
her bible and then abandoned
her faith. The house is an angry
spirit with my name on
the lease, my guests are an electrical
fire waiting to happen. Blades
like me dull if we ain't been pulled
through the throat of something
we can't name. The teenager I once was
decorated his arms with the faces
of boys that are no longer here.
But they all dead now.
I was probably inside a girl
old enough to be my reaper
when they went missing.
Sometimes a girl would call me
the wrong name because the block
was full of ghosts. Ain't nobody called
me cute until we were alone
and naked before our gods

back when I prayed to anything
that had the light pulled
violently from its body like
a harpoon. Maybe I'm someone's
great white whale, but maybe
I'm the trout that's been
thrown back so many times
the hook in my cheek is just
my cheek and I gotta tithe for
every line that gets cast down towards
my gaping mouth. I forget
every saint I've worshiped
each time I'm lifted out
of the water.

IT'S TUESDAY AND WE DIDN'T SEE ANY NEW SHOOTINGS OF BLACK PEOPLE BY POLICE TODAY SO IT'S POSSIBLE WE ARE FUCKING TONIGHT, MAYBE

I kick my daughter's / stuffed animal / out the damn
bed because it ain't / the first transgression / on our
heavily scripted / Tuesday night which doesn't / hold
any real significance / against any other / night of the

week except it's / the night my daughter / fell asleep
early, so maybe / my wife and I might / actually get
some alone time / tonight and by alone / time I mean
neither of us / will be too exhausted / to do what

gave us a / daughter in the first / place, but we got
a long way / to go considering we / can't stop laughing
that we got / a goddamn toy chest / of my daughter's
lack of clean / up under the covers / and my wife may

have rolled / over on some cookie / crumbs too, the ones
I didn't even / tell her that I gave / our daughter before
bed and she / look at me like I / hid the launch codes
from her and / I have been laughing / for five minutes

now, so my wife / puts her hand over my / mouth because if I wake
up / our daughter now, my / wife may never let me have sex / again,
so we / forgo the bed because we don't / know what else / lurks there

and instead / opt for the floor until / we both land
there hard as / reality and we both / look at each
other / in horror as we await the fruit / of our recklessness / but not a
sound comes from across

the hall so / maybe we're in the clear / except maybe
it's too quiet / now and my wife / just wants

to check / on her and I roll my / eyes even though
I was thinking / the same thing, so both / of us try to find

our clothes / which ain't hard considering / we didn't get
very far taking / them off to begin with / and we slowly
open the door / to my daughter's room / who couldn't
be more asleep / and unconcerned with / our shenanigans

but my wife lays / next to her / and rubs our daughter's back as if she /
might disappear if she stops making contact / and I lay behind / my
wife, my face buried / in her back because I am / always tired

and there's a / chance that I might / snore
and wake them both up

at least they'll know / I'm still alive

A DAY AFTER A FIGHT, MY WIFE PUTS ON HER FACE WHILE I DRIVE US TO A PARTY

I joke that I don't want to hit a bump while
driving because my wife is applying her eye–
liner with a pencil and she laughs back
that if she can do it while she is at the wheel,

then this should be no problem, and I
watch her, still carve spells around
her eyes, even as I turn on to the winding road

and maybe she just has so much practice
accounting for my lack of grace or she has accepted the risk in
performing what someone expects of her, but she doesn't flinch; not
once for the time I slam

on the brakes or the time I surrendered my stubborn body into a
vacant guest bed, not once for the fly
that spreads his entire life across the windshield
in front of my wife's evolving eyes

like me, a man still learning what death
may befall me and what gaze
I choose as moonlight for my emptying,
before the wind takes me

ANATOMY OF DAP (I)

Even when I was too dumb
to know what love sought me
without invite, I knew
that Terrell dapped me different
than the rest of the hood—fingers
of his offhand burrowed into
my shoulder while our favorite
weapons clasped each other, compressed
between our simple chests. His chin
fell upon my shoulder as if in collapse
from the journey—and this was where
he made me see him, the refusal to bury
himself in a horizon away from
my face. A lot of my brothers
filled the silence here, an audible disrupt
when we were against each other. This too
was a dance, I learned. *Ahh. Ayo. Fam. Fam.*
Everything was an alarm clock. Every siren
we placed here to warn us not to linger.
Whatever smoke a man must disperse to let
a man know this was almost over and then, we could love
each other in the withdraw, the leap away.
Our hands were still clasped, but a fist twice
the size now. *How you? Can't call it.*
I did not know what Terrell had sunk his
teeth into or whose quivering body he held
against his own the night before he held
it against mine to greet me, but I knew the
handshake was an elaborate performance
in place of saying to each other, *I'm glad we
both survived another night,* regardless
of how it birthed us.

BULLY

I don't even whup my own kid
but I've considered beating the Jesus

into this little bastard at the park when he
shoves another big-headed wobbler to

the ground. I'm not particularly religious,
either, so I'm sure Jesus seems like a weird

choice in this circumstance, but my lack
of faith doesn't make the beating I envision

less biblical. Maybe because I'm hip hop
or the ghost of a boy that used to listen to hip-hop;

in retrospect, I should say I've considered beating
the break beats into this kid, which sounds too

violent for a man that is only at this particular park
because he brought his daughter to play on the swings.

So maybe I need to chill because it's possible he's mis-
understood or the parents are terrible or he's exactly
the way the rhythm broke him and the parents are just

parents because just parents is still fucking hard.
Hopefully he's just a kid way too happy

to sit his ass down on a long piece of plastic heated
under July and burn a brand into his legs

just to feel the wind or heat or something
that isn't the touch of his parent, on his face

TONK

The summer I graduated
to the grown folk's table
was the summer when Big Roy
tried to punk me in front of LaShaun and
I swung my fist through his slick shit spitter
till I could hear his family move off the block
the following year. Later, I played Tonk
in a swamp of curses while my Uncle
told every person that walked in the room,
Did you see my nephew knock that nigga out?
and gripped my shoulder like a crane clumsily trying
to rip down a foundation, while I tried to forget
how Big Roy's teeth left the orbit of his face.
But my cousin couldn't sit with us yet,
even though he was twice my size.
Uncle said *he too soft for this grown shit,* so the next
week my cousin took the first fat joke from some
no neck junior and continued to hit him until the junior
was graduating a year later than he should've. Cousin never
spoke much after that or maybe it just seemed that way
because the phones in prison were real choppy
or maybe that's just what the rumors were
because I was too much of a coward
to visit.

THERE IS A SHAME

aimed at you
in the nerd
community if
you admit that you
like *Teen Titans Go*
almost like a betrayal
of its predecessor that
is now dead, though pre-
maturely, and never to
rise again. And I suppose
I could hide behind my
daughter's love of the
team who can't seem to
be respected enough
to be taken seriously as
my conduit into such
forbidden fanfare, but
honestly, I just enjoy
watching a Black character
like Cyborg withstanding
assaults and aggressions
and death every day
and still standing at the
end of the episode
or at least smiling through
the best laid plans of the bad
guys or who he assumes are
his allies, especially when
the only other image dragging
its bloody memory behind
my eyes is Alton Sterling's
murder like so many vacated
plots and nonsense

story endings
before him and even though
I cringe when Cyborg yells
Boo-yah, I at least know
that joy follows the sonic
boom of his call out. We
Black folk have a catchphrase
too that sounds too much
like a fired gun and our
name uttered by strangers
that miss the living version
of ourselves. Besides I can't
be concerned with what my
fellow snobs have to say about
my choice of cartoon as I lay
across the floor with my daughter
laughing because I can't guarantee
she won't see her father
on TV one day get hit
and not get
back up, and that laughter
won't become a language
she forgets in my wake.

EVEN THOUGH I LOVE YOU MORE THAN ANYTHING, THAT WON'T STOP THEM FROM KILLING YOU

is the sentence my mother leaves
off the end of each conversation like
the suffix on a boy's name whose father
is a ghost of his own making. I assume
she's watching the news again because
I saw Black people on social media say
prayers up for a sibling who I'll only know
through other people who didn't know
them. I guess the prayers rise high enough
where we broken communion wafers can't reach them,
but not high enough for management
to notice, and I assume that's got something to
do with climate change or air density or science
deniers who never seen a black body float
above a blacktop before but my mom never
says anything about praying
because we ain't all that religious. But if the
earth wants me that badly, she'll still dress in
whatever Black dress has faded the least
because we are that American and we bury
so much of ourselves just to survive each
day, so what does it matter,
if the body follows?

ANATOMY OF DAP (II)

The last time I gave Quan dap / we squared up
like pallbearers and made ourselves
big the way Black men / make everything
bigger than necessary / even though we were
already Redwoods, even / though we look
kindling to any ax / even our footwork
was mammoth when we slid into a side stance
bent at the knees / wide based like we
were straddling fresh graves / our wingspans
long and taut like a gallows' promise / because Quan
and I used to ball before we
eventually became / who we became
we add a hop to gather ourselves / in midair
for a moment / for Quan, a lifetime I guess
before we brought our hands together / hard enough
for the homies that ain't here / to laugh at how alive
we pretended to be / because LeBron and some squire
made their open hand strike sing / three times
on TV / we had two more coming that might
as well have stored creation / between the intervals
and though our shoulders / be a fast twitch ballistic
though we collect stars in each inhale / do not be fooled
when we pull our hands away / something doesn't
make it back / I coil my arm for the next swing
someone put another boy in the ground / the sting
is still fresh in my palm / a murder caws in chorus,
then falls from the sky / we yell on the second smack
like something being born / something being lit
on fire neither of us would be able to tell / the difference
perhaps we have overdone it / perhaps we outlived
our own relevance / there's no way this will end
happily, no way / we won't lose too much
in the separation this time when he loses

a sister / I gain another poem
I gained the clasp / of knowing I won't die
alone in the last act of the play / even if Quan
won't see the curtain / this time I hold
his hand like a dead man's switch / still let go
because I've never been taught any
different / except guilt is a reminder you're still
in the lottery / but now it's just me and the waiting
with Quan's / headstone on my tongue
like communion.

T'CHALLA AKA THE BLACK PANTHER HAS SEVENTEEN POEMS ABOUT BEING A FATHER

They all begin as stories of hunting with his son.

We once came upon a gazelle with a throat glistening with break...

Most of the poems are in form, rigid and always in control.
It is why he will never be a great poet.
It is why the throne has forgotten his name.

When the trappers caught me, they took my claws first...

Only one poem mentions Storm. She found it after
the tidal wave destroyed the city. After he destroyed
their marriage.

The knife pulled back the skin like an apology...

When he writes about having a son, he is writing about not having
a son. They are all poems about his father. They are all poems
about someone becoming more because someone
they loved is now dead. They are poems that don't believe
in the future.

The arrows found you first and then last.

None of the heroes that look like him were given sons, either.

*When they raised their rifles, I did not lie to you, who else could these
bullets be meant for?*

ALL APOLOGIES TO NAS

But the sunset falls through
the windshield like a new blood
and I climb the speed bumps
slow to keep us   from aging out
of the expiring day. The little
girl in the backseat is silent as the sky
that took my grandmother into its
bottomless jaw.

I can see how slumber
looks like death, where a siren that has been
shut off makes us believe that a fire
has had the air pulled from its lungs.
But, the soft burial
and then rise of an exhausted child   feels
like mending a body back together.
We arrive home and I let the car   live
for a while in the driveway because
the little girl still hasn't risen, and if this is
the cousin of death, then what must have
become of death's   father
If I can't believe in the function of smoke,
how it is evidence of a new creation before
          it rises into a larger skyline,
then I'm not sure
what the point of waking up is
or how my closing hours
into exhaustion and the promise
of rising again, help me
          forget about being so flammable.

CALL THE GOSPEL BY ITS GIVEN NAME

Before she was an egg, my daughter
was an idea that crawled down from
the roof of my mouth. If nothing else,
I can say I spoke the word of god once.
Then many times afterward.

She says grace like she's trying
to remember how my grandmother said it.
If you let your child speak in the voice
of the dead too often, hope becomes
a weather balloon you cannot keep
on the ground. She knows Jesus from
her mother, which is better than learning
about faith from me. Jesús was the store
owner that sold the older kids
loosies and gave the girls free candy
for good grades. And bad ones too.

Someone I love says they aren't having children
and I say, *I understand.* Someone questions
how can you bring
a child into this world and I picture my daughter kicking
them in the shins over and over again.

I could be more compassionate, but I was raised by the dead.
They don't have time for pretense.

I am a cathedral of scar tissue. I tackle
my daughter in the grass and she yells
again into the bloodless sky above me.
I put her to bed and remember the difference
between sleep and the kids that never
woke up. My wife catches me building gravesites
from my daughter's pillows in my sleep.

The girl does this thing where she stands
on her head while watching TV. Her legs flail
about like a helicopter above her. I'm scared
where they will lift her to, that I may not be able
to come along. I am yelling the word
of god again. I am giving god a middle
name out of frustration. Prayer works if god hears
that you used the father's tone.

My wife and daughter go through
old jewelry. It has been passed down from
the women in her family, most of them no
longer alive. My daughter wants to wear
the pearls of her great-grandmother. My daughter
wants to dress like a dead woman and suddenly,
every step I take towards her is a grave
I have to dodge. I whisk her away to the backyard
instead. I tackle her in the grass as much
as she wants. Until I am sure the ground is solid.
Until all the plots are filled
with something other than us.

THE HOMEOWNERS' ASSOCIATION WON'T LET US GROW BLACKBERRIES IN THE BACKYARD

but I remember the summer when my voice
buried the boy I had been and I spent suns

in three acres of thorns at my grandmother's
home, where the blackberries visited each July

just like her cancer. I held my weathered
and woven basket, the splintered fangs

invading my palms. My grandmother never
allowed me to pick the berries myself—

If the berries be red or purple, you just leave
them be. They ain't ripe yet. and I knew

she meant that I was done hanging with the older
boys who lived around the corner, their car

loud and alive, a thicket of smoke rising
from the doors. Grandma knew the blade

of me, knew if I could not tongue the seeds
from my teeth, I would find something

sharper. Once, one of those boys disrespected
her, and she let the pies burn in the oven

while she went outside to mark him, her palms
still stained with the morning's pickings.

That September, the cancer dragged grandma
to new hauntings. White men showed up

to her home in bulldozers and their engine
smoke swallowed the years. When they

poured the concrete over the fields, I knew
it was a tomb for the man I might have been,

for the fable that what we own belongs to us,
and even the splinters I held were not mine to keep.

WILDLIFE

I know when it doesn't flinch at my arrival,
that the rabbit in my front yard is dead. I knew

this under yesterday's sun, when the rabbit tried
to move and could do nothing but stare at me, drowning

in my merciful shadow. I have returned today
to see that my home has found death, or that death

has found the shadow I fled to. The rabbit is so small, the grass has
barely bothered to part for it. I wonder

if it will do the work for me, and pull the rabbit into itself. I've seen a
street do that. I've seen small creatures

left on a sidewalk, their bodies elongated and still until someone
confirmed that they would never pull the world

into their lungs again—and then they were gone, as if the concrete
had not been fed. But it is insatiable, the tar

and the earth and the blood it demands. I find a shovel because it is
still hot out, and my daughter will want to

play here. I assume we all dance among the dead, especially if we
don't know any better. I do not want her

to see the rabbit like this, where the rabbit is no longer
a thing but a thing left behind, but I don't

want her to not see it either. And isn't this what I went to college for?
To buy a home in a place where

my daughter can learn about death from small animals
instead of classmates? I don't know when someone she loves will

leave something behind that she
no longer recognizes. I learned that animals will flee

a scarier thing unless they have forgone fear or are already dead.
One time a police officer told

us to stop, and we ran into the arms of a new night, except for Big
Kevin, who must not have been scared,

or was already dead. Either way, the next day, he was still on the
sidewalk, and the day after that he was gone.

I do not know if the cracks of his burial took him in
or who was assigned the shovel.

THE STREET LIGHTS WATCHED MOST OF US MAKE IT HOME THAT NIGHT

The first son knows how to throw down dominoes like he is calling
for rain. If you can toss bones with
the grown folks, they might let you stay up with them
in the backyard until you can't see nothing but each other's bullshit
and laughter. They passed a curfew

two weeks back, but the old heads got gold ropes around their neck
and long braided women with thunder-laughs around their tables.
They don't have to worry about making it home cuz they already
home or already somewhere comfortable to lay their head.

I done inhaled enough smoke to make a coffin around my spirit. Bugs
stay biting my legs because to be alive means sinking your teeth into
something you presume
is already dead. One day they will be ghosts too.

Being somewhere you got no business being is the only heaven most
of us believe in. We let the darkness catch up to our youth. The
street light hums before it fully lights, it is telling us the war is still
coming, still
coming for the children. It is telling us that we
are still the children.

In Miss Greco's language arts class, she read from a knowledgeable
White man that what is most scary about the dark is the unknown, but
Black boys know exactly what the darkness wraps over its knuckles
like a prizefighter. A smile that doesn't fit our neighborhood.

The smoothed fingertips of the fathers that left their boys in the dirt
then bought new collared shirts. The second son sees his dad
whenever his mom gives the key

to a new boyfriend. His dad said something about who was or wasn't
going to do whatever in his home and now the fire marshal says no one
can live there.

Second son don't even know where he running to because home is the
twin size bed that isn't hungry that night. I'm the only boy in the crew
with a dad that cares enough to put hands on me if we make it home.
The street light lights up and somewhere my father
prepares his best suit. We buried his mother two months past but it is
dark now, and he does not know where his son is. What happens to a
man when both his legacy and memory is placed in a garden that will
never bear fruit. What to do with all these tree limbs.

As long as we on this side of I-77, we're still considered
on the south side of Akron. Which means we're still considered
missing. The third son got a brother that got into a fight at the game
and now all the Garfield High boys got a hex put on them. At least
that's what my aunt calls it. We just call it a 9 millimeter in the hands

of an angry god. The local Kings are still parked on the side streets
and we stop running. Nobody want to be confused for vengeance
tonight. Nobody want to be mixed up in ambition when the brothas
already out here ready to disappear somebody. We walk in the
blackness like there's an exit. Or an entrance. Or a ferry willing
to take the huffing breath in our chest as payment to
make it back home. But we have never been close to water. I can see
Cole Ave now, which means I can see the site of last night's war.

Fire still burning. Not true. I meant Black boy body still ain't risen
from the pavement unless you count
the paramedics that got there too late. We make a turn down the
avenue and the sidewalk begins to swallow me.
Up to the knees. None of us ever seen the desert but we know
quicksand.

First son always wears cargo pants because that's
the best place to carry his blade. He's had steel
on him ever since his sister went to a campus party
and left part of herself there. His mom said she should've been more
careful, but told us to all
be safe as we went to hang out at the house

of that man that supplies her. If you're a boy,
I guess what doesn't kill you makes you a hero
the next morning. If you're a boy, I guess what kills you
gets you a march and your mother described as graceful. The night is
so dark it looks like a curse I called a girl once. I left her parents'
home one day

saying *you'll miss me when I'm gone.* I paused
on the front steps of her porch as if this would
be the memory that haunted her. A weed grows
there now. I think she never pulled it up just to spite
me. Just to say, *now I'll never forget you because you won't leave me
alone anyway.* But isn't that what it means to be a boy who may
always reside in a body he isn't ready for? To be remembered, but not
missed? To find yourself in the dark and remember
who you cast your own darkness at? To want to find a home, any
home that will have you, any home that will hold you, and remember
what keys you lost?

Nothing else looks like a cop car when it's this dark
out. Nothing else feels like a thunderstorm of glass
when the lights turn on atop the cruiser. He is waiting for us. He is
waiting for boys that look like us.
Smell like us. Bleed like us. The loudspeaker
from the car booms:

STOP and then something else. A lot of something
else. But I don't remember. The boys disperse

the way a spider web breaks under a careless backhand. We have not
done this before, together. We have
done this before in our sleep. In the fire
drills our schools didn't teach us. My mother
won't be able to handle my burial, so I run.
I have a sister who does not know how to hate yet,
so I run. All the boys run because we are the animals they think we
are. We flee the teeth of something bigger. Something that hasn't fed.
I hear the door of the cruiser open and I am in someone's backyard. I
        hear
the door of the cruiser close and I have scaled another fence. Forgive
us, father, for we know not what our sworn protectors do. I am
running fast enough to lose years. I am running to ensure more years
        still.

I hear my own feet making a memory of the pavement and then a yell
that sounds like everybody I know.
I am still running and no one is chasing me. The yell tells me that a
hunger has been satisfied. The third son has a decisive laugh. It revs
up like an old engine,
a rolling introduction, until he is full belly, expanded chest, cackling
larger than whatever the original joke was. I can pick his laugh out of
a downpour. I can
hear his thunder over every tremor the earth dare throw at us. It is
how I mark him. It is his fingerprint.
I do not know his scream.

If someone is still pursuing, it would take years to reach me. I still
have years. I run and the third son
has no years left. I run until a pecking order
is challenged. I don't turn back and I can't place
the yell. I do not know what my own yell
sounds like either.

My uncle used to say that landmarks are for tourists
and people trying to find their way home. I can see
the street light outside of my home. I am both a tourist and a lost boy
pulling himself from the grave.
The street light is familiar in the way an uncle is,
in his favorite chair, stationed at the edge of the living
room, annoyed that you are studying him. An uncle
that made it back from war and wonders if you'll do the same tonight.
It is late, but I can see the glow
of the TV.

My father has questions and I lie. I was not the fourth son. I did not
run into a future where I doubted
its existence. I was not a ghost or a specter or almost
the reason he would have to come and get me. Or my belongings. Or
what was left, of his namesake.

BLACKEST NIGHT #6 (2010)

the rings are / just trinkets / solid, black / empty vice
without a / betrothed finger / to strangle / so I guess
death be / like that too / because a casket / just a box
until a / hero fills out / the dimensions / like air in an
ever shrinking / space / no wonder Hal / and Barry ain't
tryin' to / go back when / the rings start / whispering
nostalgia / of the empty / heartbreak / they once shared
and everybody / dead now / or dead again / I guess is
the proper / nomenclature / wouldn't want / to disrespect
the way a / white hero can / rise so quickly / from the
eternity / where the black / heroes swim / long enough
to develop / gills or schools / of tombstones
but I still / get the way / that Green Lantern / hitched a
chain around / The Flash's / chest and held on / for dear
life (for the / moment) and / let Flash enter the / speed force before
they / entered another / grave and while
I never befell an / accident that rendered / me the fastest man alive I
have run / fast enough to keep / me breathing even while my friends /
became dead and / decaying versions / of someone I once loved / and
I guess you could argue that / the heroes you once / knew are no
longer / living so what right do / you have to still be here trying to
save / a planet that will treat / your death
like a new / story arc but if a ring / comes for me,
at least / I know I've got / good company or at least
a school of / waterlogged heroes who / never
got another rebirth /

I SAY CATHEDRAL WHEN I MEAN GUNPOWDER

Over winter break, Frank put a shotgun
in his mouth and killed himself in his mother's
home which was not his home, but I can under-
stand not wanting to die in a place you're not sure

will care for your bones after you've left them.
Maybe *break* is a generous word because I was
back in the home my father had left and I was
never going back to school, but ghosts have

a way of knowing where all keys are hidden,
what kind of pacification the most guarded
beasts will submit to. It is 2 am and a person
I have left behind is telling me someone I had

lived with is trapped behind the present tense
forever. Now it is four days later and I am
in my best clothes driving into Fairfield County
where I was once called nigger on the baseball

field, where I once needed a coach to walk
with me to the bus to avoid my own purging,
and a teammate told me that it wasn't because
I was Black, but because I was that good.

Because I was not old enough to be two
things at one time yet. Frank loved Wu-Tang
and once argued me who had the best verse
on *Triumph*, but no one at this funeral knows

this story, at least not the part where Frank
kissed my forehead at a party while
we re-enacted Ghost and Rae over the music
too loud for anyone to be truly sober that night.

There is a humming here, whenever another
mourner approaches me with a trespass glare,
and I hope that Frank knows that I came here,
again, to a tree that looks at my neck and misremembers

gravity, to see him lowered into the world that
tries to claim me each and every day. I don't want
him to see me as brave, but to know that I too
understand what it means to walk into a cathedral

and hear every lock turn behind you, the stained glass
is sometimes just light born in a better neighborhood
and I can smell the gunpowder you swallowed every time I startle a
flock of birds that will never fly again.

NEW YEAR'S EVE PARTY AT ERIC'S HOUSE AND THE BLACK BOYS HAVE HAD ENOUGH

because the DJ played Doo Wop like it's brand new
even though we were 15 minutes away from 2001
and Lauren Hill baptized us over two years before
that, but this is what shedding your old coat of skin
in the suburbs looks like, pretending that you were never cut just so
you can bleed again for an audience,
and when the White boy turned his fitted cap
backwards and asked me if I had heard this song before, I didn't make
note that he was White as much as I realized how far from home I
was. And while there
was someone at the party hearing Lauren sing for her life for the first
time, there was a gathering of my blood. The song-triggered memory
of a boy who will never hear it again, a broken-necked hymn that
only wanted me to make it out of there without any scars.
The year had almost died on our skin, almost slid down our necks in
the heat of the basement filled
with people that would brag that the Blacks made it to their party, so
my friend decided we were not built to be bronzed, and grabbed his
coat on the way up the stairs.
I followed him to the Ohio wind that filled our coats.
We slid pride first into his car opening the new year
the way ungraceful fingers open a gift not meant for them. At 12:01,
my friend repeated *I can't do it, Will.*
I just can't. And I laughed. I think he meant
he couldn't go back to that party or he couldn't live
like this. If it was *I can't go back* or *I can't*
live, it wouldn't be nearly as funny.

ANATOMY OF DAP (III)

And even though I wasn't,
I still said *I'm good fam*, like

                    obedient keystrokes
          under fingers pounding away

at a problem. Make me solvable
is what I want to say, make our

               haymakers want for wind
                 without the crashing,

but I am not one to bring
a spear to a still breathing

         chest, and this pageantry loves
                me the way my father

wanted to and then didn't
so why would I bleed on

            the handshake, or the pull-in
               on the embrace, and risk

the mess of disclosure?
I am good, just not enough

        to know that I'll wake up without
          the feathers of something great

in my teeth. Every locked palm
is a prayer that gave its life for

          another voice to call its name
     and I have to assume it was someone

older that first taught me the laws
of my own body's dependence,

           probably a cousin, or someone
         we called cousin, or a stranger with

my scars, before we sewed in the
preemptive head nod, before

              we added gentle assurances
                to the silent temple that is

one Black man telling another
where to find the water, where

                                    to break open the last caged
                          borders of the ruin that brought you

MY WIFE IS SHAPED LIKE

My wife is shaped *gotdam*.
Like a coke bottle. Well, she's
Black, so actually a Pom bottle.

My wife is shaped like *good lord*.
My wife is shaped like *is she with you*, she is
shaped like lineage, like the last will be first. My

wife is shaped like *all this and natural hair too*. My
wife is shaped like *all this and a master's degree too*. She is shaped
like the planets aligning; no, my wife

is shaped like the planets getting their shit together.
My wife is shaped like *bruh, you dumb enough not
to marry this here?* She is shaped like *I ain't that dumb*.

My wife is shaped like home. She shapes me like homesick when she
is out of town. She shapes me like *I hope it's a girl*. My wife is
shaped like *do you know what*

this world does to black girls? My wife is shaped like *I've seen
enough crucifixions for one week*. My wife is
shaped like *we will never go back to Texas. Cross*

Florida off our travel plans. My wife is shaped like *don't be a martyr
on a dark freeway*. She is shaped like
a speeding ticket stays a speeding ticket.

My wife is shaped like *I married
a man, not a memorial. Not a headline.
Not another Facebook movement.*

She is shaped like
don't you dare. Don't you dare bleed out
in some car they don't think you deserve. Or on

some asphalt so hungry for your bones.
My wife is shaped like *you make it home.*
You make it home.

GREY / GRAY

Being born under a Midwestern sun means never
being guaranteed of its return. A June
overcast is the father you barely know not
coming home for a week.

Today, the sun is home and jovial and undeniable,
so we play in the backyard until I can barely breathe.

When I met my wife, we sized each other up
like Greek statues, carved from the indulgences
of others that led us here. I have forgotten most
of our mythology.

When I was young, my father would say
that sweat is earned. Now, it is a thing
I do when I try to be someone
I barely recognize.

I learn by accident the mythology of gray
sweatpants, and the exposure
of your most honest self, the usefulness
for someone else's lust. I laugh,
because it is funny, in the way that dreams
about being naked in front of a full room
of your younger self is funny.

People that love me call my weight
gain *marriage*
weight because, I am happy, after all.

I ask my friend why the sweatpants need to be gray
and she says, "There's nowhere to hide with gray."

I am the largest in the room. Always. Even
when most of me is not there.

I have as many pairs of gray sweatpants
as I have years of marriage. All of them
were bought before. None of them new
as my family.

Today, the sky looks like a thunderstorm biting its tongue. I tell
my daughter we'll play inside, even when I don't believe the rain is
coming.

My gray shirts and sweaters begin to fade to the back of my closet.
They know me too well. My body is mud and there is nowhere to hide
with gray.

My daughter pulls up my shirt, wanting to poke my stomach. She is
five, she doesn't know the old gods enough to fear them. She assumes
anything immortalized in statue is long since dead.

I haven't worn a suit in years. They fit
me like a death march.

My daughter trumpets *let me see your*
belly while we wrestle. I laugh because it's funny,
in the way that knowing the fall
will kill you well before the sudden stop, is funny.

My closet is overflowing. In my closet hang
a lot of dead men I have not written eulogies
for. I have not gotten rid of them. That is not
how I was raised to treat the departed.

My body is a June overcast. It is smoke
and the avoidance of mirrors.

It's the only sun I have room for. It is the only
sun that remembers me.

The stairs of our home have gotten steeper.
My heart is a war drum with a flaccid army
behind it. I am a lost city. The walls are tall
and hollow. I am someone's birthplace
incapable of defending itself.

My daughter asks me which is the correct
way to spell grey. I have asked this
of my own shape. Have I been misspelling
my body for years?

THREE PARTS (BLACK)
After Lauren Bullock

I.
My father is one half Chippewa, which means his mother was Black
and his father was invisible. You can see it in the way he begins to
fade from view when the dusk settles in on the boy-raised hills. First
the nose vanishes, then the ears and most of his torso until only the
night can identify his hands. But when the sun is up, his skin is a slow
cackle of flame. Snap your fingers hard enough and the cheeks of my
father will appear. Black boy sunspot. Loves the dirt. Fears being
lowered into it. Hated his father. Called his father iridescent. Called
his father *mean little Indian*. Black boy married a woman twice as
dark as him.

II.
Bird-chest son calls himself 1/4 Native. Son brag about having *Indian
in his blood*. Puffs out his chest like he done survived somethin'. Son
can't name a tribe. Son still thinks Bugs Bunny is funny. Son is 10
years old and rises with the god-rays. Son is still 1/4 on first day of
class. Still don't know what genocide means. Ain't nobody explain
erasure. Still don't know what his grandfather's real name was. Son
stole once and felt bad. Son had something taken from him and
watched the teacher not care. Son is 1/4 Native. Son gets called a
nigger on the playground and forgets fractions. Son is 1/4 I don't
remember. Son learns to walk on his phantom limbs. Son is so Black
now. Son so Black the sun shrugs. Son so Black his father can't forget
him.

III.
The not yet naked girl stares at my naked hue and asks which one of
my parents is Native American. She says she can tell by how my red
skin pushes through the shadows of the room. I always thought the
red came from anger. From the blood I could never get out of my
skin. From the rage. Or fire I haven't figured out how to control yet.

Never knew why I drink so much water and sweat curses. Never knew why I count things that burn to go to sleep. Never knew why a woman's touch on my neck felt like flint striking. Why my Black no longer has a volume knob. Ask me if I know how much Native I got in my blood and I'll tell you I tested out of math. Ask me the history of my father and I'll tell you half the story. I am the monolith or I am almost the monolith or I am swallowed under the weight of its black. If her eyes adjust to the dark, will she forget about the blood orange my chest is wrapped in?

IV.

Boy, whose child is that? That your daughter lookin' so light? Your daughter so light she gentrified the nursery? She so light look like she stole somethin' and didn't get caught. She so light her black got stretch marks. How you get a child that light, anyway? Ain't your wife darker than you? You know you married a woman same shade as your momma, right? Like half-father, like quarter-son, I guess. Your daughter light enough to have been here before. Ain't your daddy mixed with somethin' else? Ain't he Black and somethin' else? What that make you, huh? You got any room for tradition in them bones? Where you get that child from, boy? I seen your momma, she Black as oppression, I know she ain't wash up from that side of the river. You and that daughter got eyelashes long as crows' feathers. Must have gotten that from her daddy's daddy's daddy. Your wife dark enough to sing blue notes. Where you get that girl from, huh? How she get so light? What you hiding, boy? What you too ashamed to tell us?

ON THE NIGHT THAT THE CLEVELAND CAVALIERS WIN THE NBA CHAMPIONSHIP, MY FATHER'S PHONE GOES STRAIGHT TO VOICEMAIL

You've reached the phone of a consumed man
I'm sorry that I missed your call
I'm sorry that I missed your concern
I once reached for you and they put a city between us
I'm sorry the wind never calls us by the names our mothers gave us
I'm sorry I once claimed Akron and they found me bleeding
I'm sorry I was watching the game

I was watching them tear down the Rubber Bowl

I was watching them box up my youth and write Winter
across its face

I was watching the confetti fall and I remembered the hail
the cold and its familiar sharp moving up my leg

I was watching the boys crying on the hardwood floor

Like my sister cried when they put Bobby in the ground

Like my mother cried when they took her leg

I'm sorry you have to witness the hard love of my birth
I'm sorry the town is still here. We still here
I'm sorry we won

Please leave a message after the siren
Leave a message after the procession
Tell me a story of where they found you
How soft was the bed of your mother?
Tell me how she held you in a city under no clouds

Tell me how happy you are for my village
        How beautiful your wave is from so far away
Tell me again about curses
Tell me about the 50 years of not winning
        eating
        being broken across the lap of a lover
Please leave a message after the curse
Please leave your well wishes in deeper tombs
Please leave

INHERITANCE

My father is a brilliant man who still
doesn't understand the opera. He doesn't listen
to rap, but can pull glass from every wound they
describe. He enters my home standing under
the portraits of his daughter-in-law and his only grandbaby and
cannot comprehend why
I don't keep a gun. My father was a man once
my age, told to protect everything while being
told that nothing actually belonged to him,
not even the smoke of his burning house
or the open hand of his father. Now, my father's
voice is a hammer he tries not to swing.
My father's hands are fog and mist collecting
on the windows. He doesn't understand why I
ever leave the house to march. He doesn't
understand why anyone younger than me still
has to. The news is on and my father sighs out
loud to remember that the act of breathing
is something he paid an expensive mortgage
for. My father once told me the only thing he liked
about the city more than the country is that they
will find your remains quicker. My father sees
my neighborhood and asks where all the trees are.
He scoffs that I want to finish our basement, can't understand why I
would volunteer to be in the ground. He is not a superstitious man but
that doesn't mean
he doesn't believe in curses or blood omens
or wearing a hooded shirt under a hungry sky or politics you don't
have to dig into the earth for. He mocks survival when the thing that
has tried to kill him
is still alive too. Maybe my father's version
of the future is where he forgets what the past
tried to do to him. Maybe my father is still healing

from the years that tried to set him on fire
or the redlining that underlined his surname
or the afro he wore that a man once grabbed
a fistful of and pulled off a bus. My father grew
up in Ohio and doesn't understand why the South is supposed to scare
him. I try to talk to my father
about the election and my heavy eyes and who
is coming for us, and who will try to leave us among
the other dying things and he just shakes his head.
Slow. The way the breeze rocks something from one side to the other,
a wind chime so heavy it doesn't even make a sound.

I MIGHT BE WRONG

but in every photograph we share, my father is never
still. My seventh birthday. Easter of '94, the last
Christmas. I pick up the picture of my sister's

graduation, the worn frame splinters
my palm in fidelity to him. There is a wealth
of sky in each scene. Was he always trying

to escape to the marginalia? If the instinct of man
is to return home, then what would make me
untenable? At my wedding, he shrinks

in my shadow. In the photo, I am wearing
his watch which fled into the years
too. Maybe he took it back after he took

back his vows to my mother. Maybe it sits
in a box, some quiet part of the house
I haven't visited, a perfect dust collected

and untouched, safe from my hands. It isn't
enough that I wear his eyes. His clean scalp.
His aversion to locks. I visit him outside

the city, his home on silent acres. This will be
yours, he says, his voice echoing among
the empty trees. I have been here before.

On his land. My living room. Have I found
the sky in my own photos, a balloon
around my daughter's wrist?

ON TRESPASSING

I realize too late
that the *Lion King*
joke I make to my father
as we stand

adrift in our own sweat
and haggard breath
on his modest acres
only works after he dies.

I will be left to figure
out how to bring earth
to my lips when I never
courted it. I will

have no idea what to
do with it, having lived
so far away from my
father's heart, how do I

sink my hands into this
dirt when it took them
so long to learn his frayed

edges and what bones
were still worth the scars?
I have no idea what

I will do with my father's
body, what ground respects
tradition enough
to place my father

in itself before my
own feckless song, a prisoner
pushing out from my tired
skin, trying to hold me

into a bundle worthy
of inheriting a land he has
bled for simply because
I inherited his blood.

If I am not allowed to
make this joke here, I do
not know what other
country will have me.

I am alive
and my father's gifts
will exist when he
no longer will.

This is a land
with my name on its
borders, the same fences
that cut through my

nuclear family, the same
soil under my feet when
I remember what ground
will be good enough to take
my father someday.

BRAND NEW

Maybe I am the nigga my father warned me about, blue as a bruise
standing on the palms of dead things, house erected from my back
and flapping in moth frenzy. I have cut down the trees. Let my
daughter play below the UV rays; maybe I was supposed to be a
lumberjack or a loaded insult in someone else's grip, something my
white neighbors would think is dangerous, but too honorable to fear.
Maybe I'm living a life with the monogram of someone with more
gravity above my head but now that I'm here, I won't settle my bones
in a hood without sidewalks anymore. But ain't that the gospel of the
blade and what part of the body is left to be preserved in amber?
Because something made from me gotta outlive me, right? Something
has to find a quiet spot in the world and call it theirs and not die until
dying ain't really a thing we do anymore. Maybe that's supposed to be
my child, but I too am someone's legacy and that ain't made the
bullets any slower. I gave my apex years to a woman who might
remember me, and my wife got what was left. I pick at the grey hairs
in my beard and three black strands come off in my fingers like the
last supper. Guess old is a thing you ain't until you are and then you
never not that until you no longer that either. And my father just
laughs at how my lawn is green as a new soldier but I can't stop the
weeds from growing all big like the end of everything.

STILL CAN'T DO MY DAUGHTER'S HAIR

It is as shameful as it is a relief. I don't know
how to make her more. I reach for her and don't know
how to dull my edges. I fear her scalp
will know I'm a fraud. Will declare my trespass, search
for water and find me the shipwreck.
I clutch her like a blessing I once stole. My blood is
a graceless dancer. My hands are petty prayers. Hold her
like a clumsy ponytail. Like the curtain holds
the wind and its violent song.

I fear that I am not enough. That I am water,
but not enough. I fear the drowning. What I will find
among the ocean floor. My daughter loves me
and a crow is released from my throat. My daughter misses me and I
am not worthy. I am not here. Some nights, I kiss her goodnight and
my jaw unhinges.
Some nights I tuck her in and my fingers become ash.

I leave the house and her voice changes in my head.
It surprises me when I hear it in person. I am boarding
a plane that does not lead back to her. I enter a city where she has
never drawn a breath. I read a poem, about my daughter and a glass
falls from the bar.
This is not a metaphor for what I have lost.
I am afraid of the tide.

Someone calls me a good man and my daughter coughs herself
awake. Pull strands of my daughter's
hair from between my teeth.
I have nightmares, where my daughter forgets my face.
Thinks I am the sun and waits for nightfall.

I have nightmares, where my only child is a boy who is just like me. I
have nightmares about the sky.

How it looms over me like a flood. I am sleeping
and a child cries in the night. I wake up and she is three years older. I
wake up alone in a limitless ocean.
There is a child crying from the shore. I do not know
if she is crying out for me.
I have forgotten my own name.

GIGI

My wife is talking in the living room
lost in memory when she mentions

her grandmother. Our daughter
informs us that Gigi is

dead and of course she
is because this is the cost of us

getting old like White folks. *Gigi
is dead though* and the five-year-old

isn't sad, but merely broadcasting
necessary information, even when

the tears of Gigi well under my wife's
eyes and she says to our excited child

Yes, Gigi passed away, sugarplum
and plum returns, *does pass away*

mean dead? Of course, she is her
father's daughter and often

only asks the questions that the living
can't answer. But my wife

is patient. Still loves the world more
than my past allows me to, and simply.

nods to keep from dripping onto the floor.
I just stare at the girl, who can only be

my brightly stitched heart, who shrugs
at death when she hasn't seen it

like her father has. Maybe I will spend
my chest empty trying to keep her

an obelisk, only for my passing to be
the thing that breaks her. Maybe I miss

boys whose faces I can barely
remember. Maybe my face was once a

different boy, untouched by razor and
nightfall. I kneel close to her, her heart

steady and rhythmic. An uneventful chorus.
I ask, *Do you miss Gigi?* And she

says, *Yeah,* the way I answer a new
sunlight by squinting at its existence

ACKNOWLEDGMENTS

I will never do justice to name everyone that has been instrumental in helping to inspire the work contained in this collection. However, I need to specifically thank Mahogany L. Browne, Airea Dee Matthews, Barbara Fant, and Nicole Homer for making me want to write poems worthy of their affection. I can only hope that I have not wasted their tireless efforts and investment in me.

I would also like to thank the journals that published versions of the following poems when they were just orphans in the wild, before finding a home together under the same roof. Thank you.

Wildlife
Adroit Journal

Biology
Pack
Beechstreet Review

Found
Three Parts (Black) after Lauren Bullock
Tonk
Drunk In The Midnight Choir

Blackest Night #6 (2010)
T'Challa Has Seventeen Poems About Being a Father
Freezeray Poetry

I Turn the Volume Down Because Beyoncé Says Fuck While I Drive My Daughter to School
Muzzle

Dust
The Offing

I Say Cathedral When I Mean Gunpowder
Rattle

Jasmine, Wherever
Winter Tangerine

ABOUT THE AUTHOR

William Evans is a writer and nerd connoisseur from Columbus, OH. He represented Columbus at the National Poetry Slam a total of eight times and appeared on a Finals stage at the national level on three separate occasions. He is the founder of the Writing Wrongs Poetry Slam, an author of three poetry manuscripts, a Callaloo Fellow and a recipient of the Sustainable Arts Grant.

William is also the co-founder and editor-in-chief of BlackNerdProblems.com, a pop culture website and community that serves as an unapologetic space for intersectional nerddom.

OTHER BOOKS BY BUTTON POETRY

If you enjoyed this book, please consider checking out some of our others, below. Readers like you allow us to keep broadcasting and publishing. Thank you!

Aziza Barnes, *me Aunt Jemima and the nailgun.*

J. Scott Brownlee, *Highway or Belief*

Nate Marshall, *Blood Percussion*

Sam Sax, *A Guide to Undressing Your Monsters*

Mahogany L. Browne, *smudge*

Neil Hilborn, *Our Numbered Days*

Sierra DeMulder, *We Slept Here*

Danez Smith, *black movie*

Cameron Awkward-Rich, *Transit*

Jacqui Germain, *When the Ghosts Come Ashore*

Hanif Willis-Abdurraqib, *The Crown Ain't Worth Much*

Aaron Coleman, *St. Trigger*

Olivia Gatwood, *New American Best Friend*

Donte Collins, *Autopsy*

Melissa Lozada-Oliva, *peluda*

William Evans, *Still Can't Do My Daughter's Hair*

Rudy Francisco, *Helium*

Available at **buttonpoetry.com/shop** and more!